acknowledgements

These quotations were gathered lovingly but unscientifically over several years and/or were contributed by many friends or acquaintances. Some arrived-and survived in our files-on scraps of paper and may therefore be imperfectly worded or attributed. To the authors, contributors and original sources, our thanks, and where appropriate, our apologies.
-The Editors

credits

Compiled by M.H. Clark.
Designed by Steve Potter.

ISBN: 978-1-935414-01-8

1st Printing.
Printed with soy ink in China.

It's *your* day!

Compiled by M.H. Clark
Designed by Steve Potter

May only *good* things come your
way every moment of *today.*

-UNKNOWN

Celebrate we will, because life is
short but *sweet* for certain.

-DAVE MATTHEWS

Good old days start with good

new days like *today.* -DENISE SETTLE

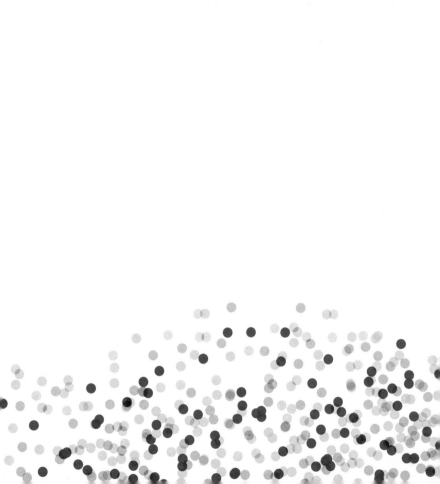

...the *good life* is waiting for us— here and now. -B.F. SKINNER

Whatever you're ready for
is ready for you.

-MARK VICTOR HANSEN

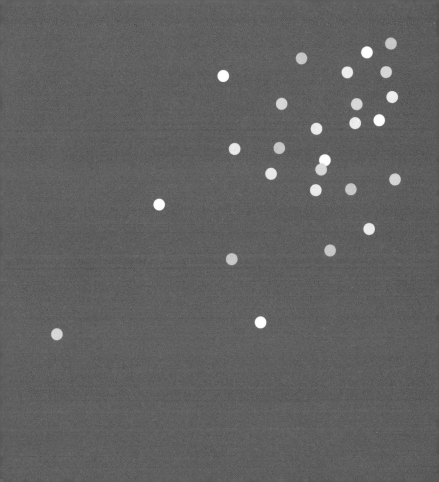

Celebrate your existence! -WILLIAM BLAKE

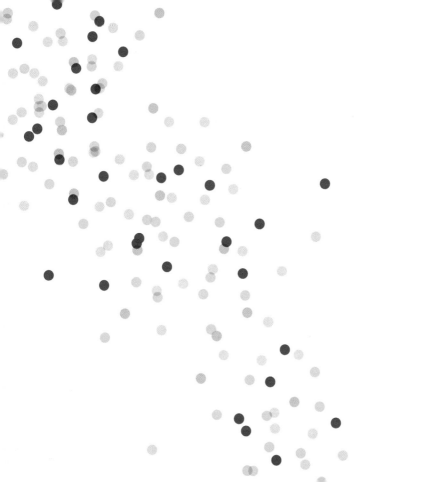

Life is a *promise* Fulfill it.

-MOTHER TERESA

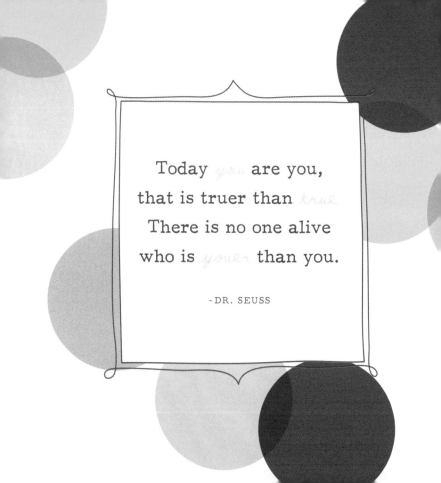

Today you are you,
that is truer than true
There is no one alive
who is youer than you.

- DR. SEUSS

I *finally* figured out the only reason

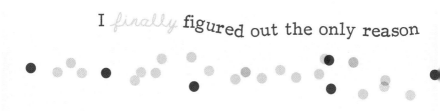

to be *aline* is to enjoy it. — RITA MAE BROWN

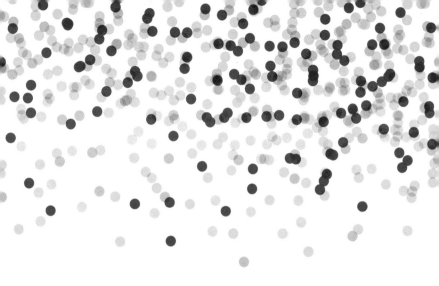

The more you praise and *celebrate* your life,

the more there is in *life* to celebrate.

-OPRAH WINFREY

The *best* is yet to be. -ROBERT BROWNING

There is always one
*moment*...when the
door **opens** and lets the
future in.

-GRAHAM GREENE

I shall make
of *this day*—
each moment of
this day–a heaven on
earth. This is *my day*
of opportunity.

-DAN CUSTER

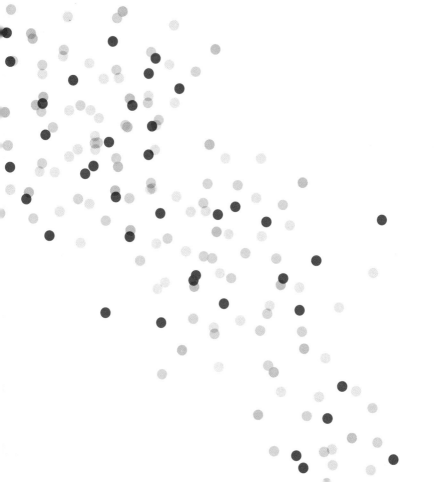

We do *contain*
within ourselves
*infinite* possibilities.

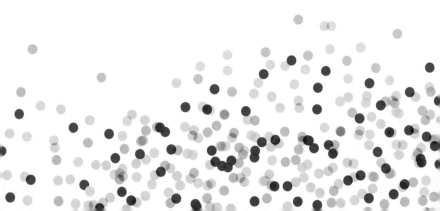

*Let us* do something today which the
world may talk of *hereafter.*

-CUTHBERT COLLINGWOOD

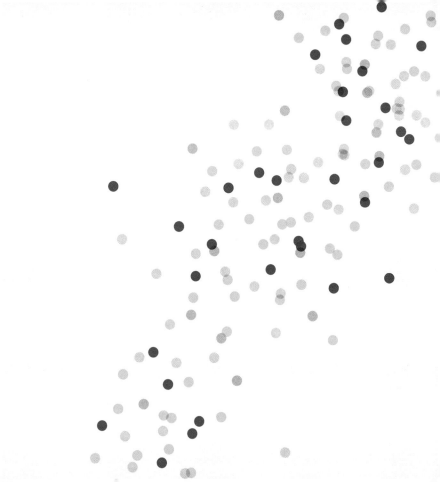

Cherish yesterday. Dream tomorrow.

*Live* like crazy **today.**

-UNKNOWN

Dream no *small* dreams...

-JOHANN WOLFGANG VON GOETHE

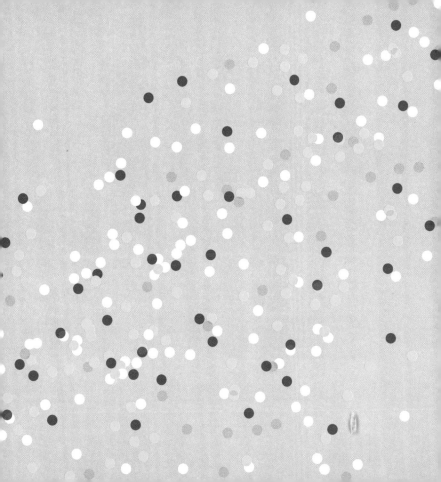

...hear and enjoy
*life's* music
everywhere.

THEODORE FONTANE

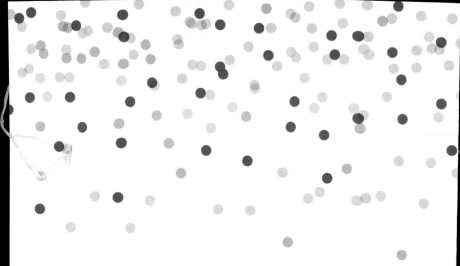

The beginning is *always* today.

-MARY WOLLSTONECRAFT

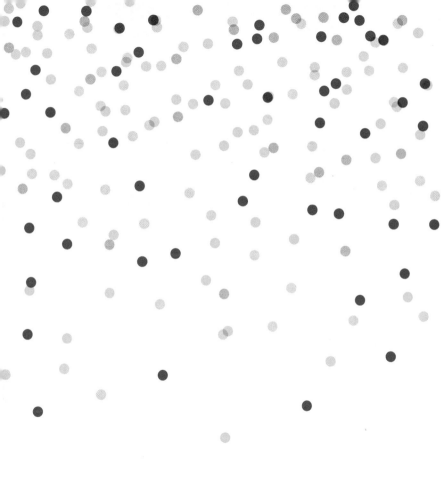

Pop the cork and tip the glass,

and *drink* the moment.

-MARIE VON EBNER-ESCHENBACH